Mastering the Art of Inner peace

A Practical Guide to Stoicism

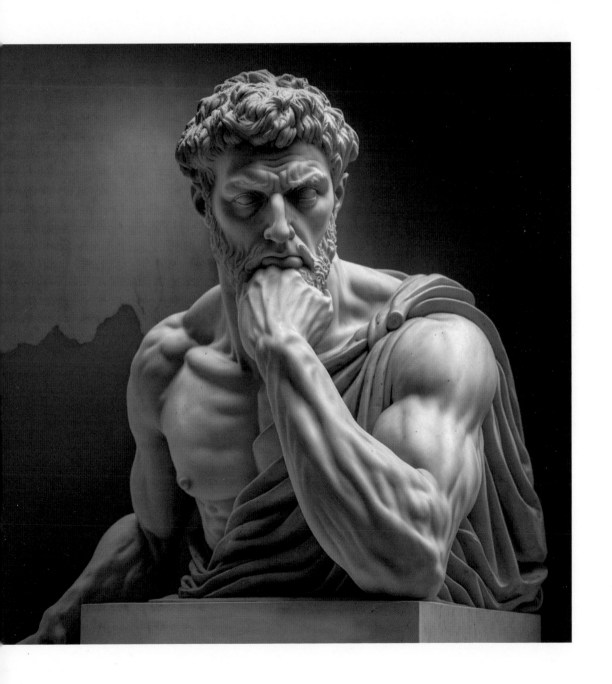

Content

Introduction

Stoicism is a school of thought that was founded by Zeno of Citium in the 3rd century BC. The Stoics were a school of thought that flourished in Ancient Greece and Rome. It teaches the development of self-control and fortitude as a means of overcoming destructive emotions. It was one of the most influential philosophical movements of the Hellenistic period. The Stoics believed in using reason and logic to examine the world and make decisions. They believed in self-control, living in harmony with others, and making reasonable judgements.

The Stoics were some of the most influential thinkers of their time. And their teachings are just as relevant today as they were over 2,000 years ago.

written by Tyronne Morrison

In this guide, we're going to explore what Stoicism is, its fundamental principles, and how you can use it to improve your life. The Stoics believed that by mastering one's emotions, one could achieve a life of harmony, wisdom, and virtue. They believed that the best way to achieve this was to live in accordance with nature.

Stoicism has resurfaced in recent years as a popular philosophy for dealing with the challenges of modern life. The Stoics offer a refreshing perspective on how to deal with difficult situations and find peace of mind.

In this guidebook we will explore some ancient tips for living a Stoic life.

1. What is Stoicism?

In the modern era, Stoicism has been reconsidered for its potential applications to the challenges of everyday life. While Stoicism itself has gone through various changes over the centuries, the underlying philosophy remains the same: that we can live more peacefully and harmoniously by mastering our passions and attitude towards life.

The Stoic teachings emphasise the belief that true happiness and tranquillity come from accepting and understanding the transitory nature of the material world. The Stoic life is a path of inner development rather than an exercise in external accomplishments.

They also believe in using reason and understanding to take control of our lives. This involves developing an inner independence from circumstance and learning how to free yourself from the tyrannical emotions of fear, anger, and joy.

Practising Stoic philosophy involves looking inward, being aware of our thoughts and emotions, and being mindful of the present moment. It also involves cultivating a sense of equanimity or balanced response to external events and people, rather than reacting impulsively to changes. Additionally, the Stoics promote the importance of living a simple, honest life and striving for moral excellence.

2. The Stoic Philosophy

The Stoic philosophy asserts that true human happiness is only attainable by living a virtuous life. Broadly speaking, this means showing restraint and exercising self-control to resist the vicissitudes of fortune and the associated suffering. Furthermore, a virtuous life involves the practice of moral behaviour based on wisdom, courage, and justice, within the present experience.

written by Tyronne Morrison

At its core, Stoicism is based on the concept that the path to combating the vicissitudes of life is found within the individual, not beyond them. Given the changing nature of the world and our inability to control external situations, Stoics rely on managing their own responses and inner thoughts in order to live in harmony with the world and its natural order.

The Stoics also believed that a life lived in accordance with our ethical principles can lead to a life of contentment and joy, regardless of our external circumstances. To follow this philosophy, the Stoics suggest training and conditioning our minds to think and respond accurately, so that external events are viewed objectively and handled with the right attitude.

In summary, the Stoic philosophy suggests that by training our minds and controlling our emotions, we can ultimately lead a more fulfilled and meaningful life.

Guidelines for living an ethical life

written by Tyronne Morrison

3. The Stoic Way of Life:

To embody a Stoic life, it is important to find the middle path, between overindulgence and total abstinence. This involves following a few basic guidelines for living an ethical life:

1. Practice self-control: Stoic philosophers believed that it is important to control oneself and learn to be independent to ensure growth and resilience in life.

2. Value indifference: Stoics strive to be indifferent to events and situations, as they believe that this will give us greater control over our life.

3. Practice non-attachment: Stoics believe it is important to detach oneself from external stimuli, to recognise that all things are transitory and to remain resistant to any external influences.

4. Cultivate equanimity: The Stoic way of life means achieving a sense of balance and calmness, even in the midst of chaos and turmoil. The practice of Stoicism is about finding the middle path between extremes and aiming for mental balance.

5. Find solace in overcoming adversity: Stoics believe that facing and enduring hardships is an essential part of our development. They advocate practising resilience in order to remain present and accept whatever life throws our way.

6. Create meaningful connections: Stoics suggest that we seek to foster meaningful and intimate relationships with people.

4. The Stoic Attitude (Ancient Tips)

The Stoic attitude involves understanding the difference between what one can change and what one cannot change. Stoics believe it is important to accept what fate has for us and to make the most of what we can control. This is a key part of their philosophy, as it encourages us to practise a mind-set of unwavering mental toughness and resilience. Here are some ancient tips for developing and maintaining a Stoic attitude:

1. Exercise control over your will: The Stoic attitude involves learning to prioritise tasks and actions that bring us closer to our goals. By exercising control over our will, we can become more aware of our purpose and stay on track accordingly.

2. Cultivate resilience: Stoics believe it is important to cultivate resilience in order to stay focused, remain present and accept whatever life throws our way.

3. Re-purpose emotions: Stoics recommend recognising and using feelings as part of an experience, rather than letting emotions take over completely in order to gain clarity.

4. Develop a growth mindset: The Stoic attitude involves developing a growth mindset and continuously learning over the course of life. This encourages us to see challenges as opportunities for growth and to maintain a balanced view of life.

5. Maintain a long-term perspective: To keep a Stoic attitude, it is important to maintain a long-term perspective and evaluate the consequences before making decisions. This helps us to avoid rash and impulsive behaviour by identifying the bigger picture.

5. The Stoic Mindset: (Ancient Tips)

Stoics believe it is important to cultivate a Stoic mind set in order to stay focused, remain present and accept whatever life throws our way. This can be done by developing and practising the following habits:

1. Focus on the present: The Stoic attitude involves learning to focus on the present without worrying about the past or the future. This helps us to keep our minds clear and concentrate on the task at hand.

2. Practice self-reflection: Self-reflection involves examining our thoughts and behaviours, understanding what motivates us and developing strategies to improve ourselves.

3. Value yourself: The Stoic attitude encourages us to value ourselves by focusing on our own thoughts and feelings, rather than on what others think and how we measure up in society.

4. Focus on the process: Stoics recommend focusing on the process, rather than on the ultimate goal, in order to stay motivated and stay in the moment.

5. Ask questions: The Stoic attitude involves asking ourselves questions, such as "What should I be aware of?" and "How can I use this knowledge to improve my situation?", in order to gain perspective and clarity.

5. Avoid judging yourself: The Stoic mind set discourages us from judging ourselves or our actions, instead helping us to practise self-acceptance and understanding.

6. The Stoic Goals

The Stoics believed that life was complex and its true understanding was beyond our knowledge. Therefore, they set out to make life less complex by setting goals that were in agreement with nature. The Stoics identified 4 main goals:

1. Wisdom: To attain a deep understanding of life and reality.

2. Courage: To act courageously in uncertain and challenging situations.

3. Justice: To act justly and morally, guided by principles of fairness and equality.

4. Moderation: To temper our urges and desires, achieving harmony in thought and action.

These four goals provided the Stoics with a framework to live a meaningful life, free from suffering and full of self-actualisation. By following these Stoic goals and cultivating a Stoic mind set, the modern Stoic can live a life of peace, purpose, and utility.

7. The Stoic Virtues

The Stoics also laid out four virtues to be cultivated in order to attain the goals of a meaningful Stoic life. These virtues are:

1. Wisdom: Self-reflection, openness to new knowledge and understanding.

2. Justice: Integrity and a fair-mindedness in all dealings.

3. Courage: Defiance in the face of fear and uncertainty.

4. Temperance: Moderation in thought, action and emotion.

These virtues are the foundations of Stoicism and enable the modern Stoic to serve the greater good. By following the Stoic virtues and applying their philosophies, Stoics can live a life of purpose and value. Whether it's a small step, like resisting the temptation of a life of chaos and seeking out order, or a big one, like standing up for what is right, Stoic virtues provide the strength to act and to pursue a life of service and peace.

8. The Stoic Practices

The Stoics believed that certain practices, if cultivated as habits, can cultivate Stoic virtues.

1. Practising Self-Control: Controlling one's emotions, reactions and urges can help to improve the ability to move away from negative impulses and towards motivations and actions of true value.

2. Seek Out Wisdom: Embrace knowledge and learning. Read and study great works, travel and observe. Build a strong moral foundation by exploring the theories and philosophies of the ancients.

3. Act With Altruism: Whenever possible, act with the greater good in mind. Consider how your actions may affect others and take responsibility for the consequences of your decisions.

4. Meditation and Reflection: Reflection and contemplation on the Stoic principles, virtues, and on one's own life can help to make the right decisions when challenged with the difficult choices.

5. Speak Carefully and Listen Intently: The Stoics believed in carefully considering one's words before they are spoken and to be open to different perspectives.

The Stoic virtues and practices, when taken to heart and actively applied, are powerful tools to make meaningful changes in one's life, and to live with purpose.

How To Be Stoic: 7 steps

1. The Stoic Attitude

The Stoic attitude is the philosophy that one should always maintain a calm, dispassionate attitude in the face of adversity. This means not reacting impulsively or in haste. Instead, one should stay centred and focused on the facts in order to make the best decisions.

The Stoic attitude is about being conscious of your inner thoughts and feelings. This requires being mindful and reflective of your inner being. By becoming aware of your feelings and not allowing them to control you, you can cultivate a Stoic attitude.

2. Live in the Present

written by Tyronne Morrison

The only thing that is certain is change, and the past and future are outside one's control. Therefore, one should live in the present moment and take action accordingly.

This means being mindful of present experiences and focusing on today's tasks and how they relate to achieving long-term goals. It also means taking time to appreciate the present moment and enjoying the beauty in life without worrying too much about the future.

The Stoic attitude encourages one to make wise and conscious decisions in the present, using the past only as a reference. This includes being aware of one's behaviours and choosing those which are mindful and beneficial.

Furthermore, living in the present also means living with a sense of abundance. This means having a positive outlook and being grateful for the gifts that life brings. Being aware of the present allows one to better appreciate the things we already have, and accept any hardships or successes as part of life's journey.

Finally, the idea of living in the present means free from worries of the future or regretting decisions of the past. We should strive to find balance between the two, enjoying the present and planning for the future.

3. Use your Impressions

Another important part of being Stoic is learning to cultivate one's impressions about things. This means recognising our initial perspective towards various people, events, or even situations and attempting to analyse these impressions and hone them further.

A Stoic's goal is to ask oneself: What is my impression of this event/person/situation? Does it fulfil my need of living a virtuous or meaningful life? Am I being too judgemental or do I lack enough evidence to form an opinion?

The most important part of cultivating impressions is to not make any immediate decisions when faced with a new person or experience but, instead, take some time to reflect on it and its consequences on our lives. Making sure each choice we make is well-formed and weighed against our internal values and its potential impact.

This practice serves as a reminder to us that it is important to take some pause, step back, and reflect on our decisions and how it will affect our lives. Our first impressions are not always the best ones, and most times our deliberation and contemplation can help us lead better and more meaningful lives.

4. Follow nature

Nature is a great teacher for Stoics, who learn to observe nature's rhythms and cycles, which has led to the development of concepts such as the harmony of nature, the unity of all things, and the divine spark of life. It is suggested that Stoics see themselves as a tiny part of the grand wildlife, expressing feelings of awe for the universe and their place in it.

Apart from reflection and contemplation, this practice of following nature also involves participating in physical activities like hiking and camping which provide a refreshing perspective and help to boost mental well-being. This also teaches us how to be mindful of the present by releasing us from constant worries, anxieties, and stress.

We can also learn to be patient and resilient by observing plants that sprout, bloom, and eventually die after a lifetime of service. The same lessons may be learned by observing animals, the warmth of fire, and even the clouds that sweep the sky.

Stoics believe that by giving ourselves to nature, it helps us to become better human beings. Nature can help us learn more about our strengths and weaknesses and how even the smallest details make for a better way of life. This also develops our sense of hope and understanding which becomes essential when facing tough times.

5. Cultivate apatheia

Apathy or 'apatheia' is another important teaching in Stoic philosophy; apatheia is often compared to being indifferent or unaffected by emotions. It does not mean a lack of feeling for others or for one's self-interest, but rather a lack of being overly concerned with a situation.

Learn apatheia by observing nature. Be accepting of things as they are and realise they are out of our control. This means that we should neither embrace nor reject something that happens to us, or give too much or too little emotional attention to the situation. Instability and insecurity can be avoided by cultivating feeling less rather than more.

This approach of apatheia helps to prevent emotional outbursts and emotional suffering; it does not mean you must become emotionless. Instead, you must be emotional in a mindful manner, respectful of your own emotional needs and respectful of the needs of other people. Apatheia also helps in preserving freedom of choice by removing an impediment to sound judgement.

6. Seek Wisdom and Live Virtuously

Wisdom is attained through studying and understanding the natural order of the universe. This includes understanding how to align our wants and desires with what the universe deems as just.

Living Virtuously involves aligning one's behaviour, desires and thoughts with values that are compatible with those of Stoic philosophy. This involves living responsibly and tackling challenges, both moral and physical, with equanimity, using reason instead of emotion as a guide, and cultivating virtue as the highest goal in life.

It also involves gaining insight into the larger purpose of life, including understanding one's place in the grand scheme of things, and realising that nature has appointed us for a purpose – that of contributing to the good of the universe in one way or another. To maintain virtue, Stoics try to live in a manner that is consistent with nature, and work hard to remove bad habits, always striving to improve themselves.

7. Death is not to be feared

Once one understands the nature of the universe and their place within it, death no longer needs to be feared. For the Stoic, death should not be seen as a punishment but rather as a natural occurrence. It is part of the cycle of life, and it is ultimately inevitable for all of humanity.

written by Tyronne Morrison

The Stoic perspective encourages us to live without fear of death. Rather than fight against it, we should accept it and embrace it. In the ancient texts, this is signified by the phrase "memento mori" or remember that you have to die. In other words, we are reminded to make the most of our lives and to live towards bringing benefit to ourselves and others.

By recognising death as a normal part of life, we can take a serene perspective on our lives and be ready when it comes. We can love, learn and eventually pass on our knowledge to others, knowing that whatever happens in our lives or after our death, the universe will still continue ticking along.

Wrap Up: How To Be Stoic

Finally, in order to wrap up the Stoic steps, one must learn to abide by the Stoic principles of temperance, prudence and justice. These principles are based on living with personal integrity, maintaining mental clarity, and making decisions in a wise and rational manner.

Temperance is about controlling one's desires and appetites, in order to achieve self-control and inner freedom from external influences. Prudence means constantly looking ahead and learning from one's mistakes, while keeping in mind the consequences of one's actions. And justice is being fair and just at all times, giving others credit where it's due and striving to do what is right, even when it isn't easy.

By following these Stoic principles, one can strive towards improving oneself and eventually have the courage and strength to face life's circumstances with ease. Adopting a Stoic mindset will help us live a more meaningful and fulfilling life

Stoicism and meditation

toicism and meditation are two practices that can be complementary to each other. Stoicism is a hilosophy that emphasises personal ethics, rationality, and virtue as guideposts for leading a ulfilled life. Meditation, on the other hand, is a practice that cultivates mindfulness, awareness, nd inner peace.

toicism encourages us to develop an inner resilience and mental toughness to face the challenges f life. Meditation can help us to cultivate this resilience by teaching us how to manage our houghts and emotions, and detach ourselves from negative feelings.

toicism also places a great emphasis on the present moment and focusing on what is within our ontrol. Meditation similarly encourages us to be present and mindful, to live in the present moment rather than getting lost in thoughts about the past or worries about the future.

3y combining the practices of stoicism and meditation, we can develop a greater mental strength and resilience, allowing us to live a more fulfilling life with greater control over our thoughts and emotions.

Regularly practising meditation, individuals can learn to observe and identify their emotional states in the present moment without judgement. This can help individuals to respond to their emotions in a more mindful and intentional way, rather than reacting impulsively.

Furthermore, meditation also lowers the activity in the amygdala, a region in the brain that is responsible for the processing of emotions such as fear and anxiety. As a result, regular meditation can decrease the intensity of emotional responses to stimuli and help individuals to develop greater emotional regulation and control.

Overall, through cultivating mindfulness and emotional regulation, meditation can be an effective tool for managing and controlling one's emotions.

A guide on how to meditate successfully!

1. Find a quiet and comfortable space: Choose a place where you won't be disturbed, and where you feel comfortable sitting for a period of time. You can sit on a cushion or a chair, whichever is more comfortable.

2. Sit comfortably: Find a comfortable seated position with good posture. Keep your back straight, your shoulders relaxed, and your hands resting on your knees or in your lap.

3. Focus on your breath: Close your eyes and focus on your breath as it moves in and out of your body. Allow your breath to be your anchor and your guide throughout your meditation practice.

4. Let your thoughts come and go: Your mind will inevitably wander, and that's okay. When you notice your mind wandering, simply acknowledge the thought and then return to focusing on your breath.

5. Try guided meditations: If you find it difficult to focus, you can try guided meditations. There are many apps and websites that offer guided meditations, so you can choose one that resonates with you.

6. Set a timer: Start with a short meditation session, such as 5 or 10 minutes, and gradually work your way up to longer sessions. Use a timer so you know when your session is over.

7. Make meditation a daily habit: The more you practise, the easier it will become. Try to make meditation a daily habit, even if it's just for a few minutes each day.

8. Remember, meditation is a practice that takes time and patience to develop. Don't worry if you find it difficult at first – keep trying! With practice and consistency, you'll start to experience the many benefits of meditation.

Breath-work Meditation

Breath-work is a type of meditation practice that involves intentionally controlling your breath to produce certain effects on your mental, emotional or physical state. Breath-work can be incredibly powerful and transformative.

Breath-work has been shown to have many benefits for overall health and well-being, including:

- Reducing stress and anxiety: By intentionally controlling your breath, you can help reduce the levels of stress hormones in your body and induce a calming and relaxing effect.

- Boosting energy levels: When you practise breath-work, you're getting more oxygen into your body, which can increase your energy levels and help you feel more alert and awake.

- Enhancing mental clarity and focus: Breath-work can help increase focus and improve mental clarity by calming the mind and reducing distracting thoughts.

- Improving sleep quality: Breath-work has been shown to help regulate the nervous system and promote relaxation, making it an effective tool for improving sleep quality and reducing insomnia.

- Enhancing physical performance: By improving oxygenation of the body, breath-work can help enhance physical performance, endurance and recovery from exercise.

- Reducing symptoms of depression and anxiety: Practising breath-work can help reduce symptoms of depression and anxiety. Studies have shown that breath-work can increase feelings of well-being and improve mental health.

- Strengthening the immune system: Breath-work can help strengthen the immune system by reducing stress and inflammation in the body.

These are just a few of the many benefits of breath-work. Incorporating a regular breath-work practice into your daily routine can have powerful effects on your overall health and well-being.

A brief guide to breath-work:

1. Find a comfortable seated position: Sit in a comfortable position with your back straight and your feet on the ground. You can sit on a cushion or a chair, whichever is more comfortable.

2. Begin with deep belly breaths: Take a few deep breaths, filling your lungs completely and expanding your belly as you inhale. Exhale slowly and deeply, fully releasing all the air from your lungs.

3. Choose a breath-work technique: There are many different techniques for breath-work, but a basic one you can try is called "4-7-8" breath. Breathe in for 4 counts, hold for 7 counts, and exhale for 8 counts. Repeat this cycle for several minutes or until you feel a shift in your body.

4. Focus on your breath: As you practise breath-work, focus your attention on the sensations of your breath. Notice how the breath moves in and out of your body, and try to stay present with each inhale and exhale.

5. Be aware of emotions and sensations: As you continue your breath-work practice, pay attention to any emotions or sensations that arise in your body. Simply observe them without judgement or attachment.

6. End with some minutes of quiet breathing: When you're finished with your breath-work, take a few more deep breaths and allow yourself to relax into a state of calm and stillness.

7. Breath work is a self-regulating practice, if you feel any physical or emotional discomfort, pause or stop the exercise and return to a natural breathing pattern.

Conclusion

written by Tyronne Morrison

stoicism can offer a valuable framework for living a fulfilling and purposeful life. By focusing on what is within our control and accepting what is outside of our control, we can cultivate inner peace, resilience, and happiness. Through the practical applications of Stoic principles of wisdom, justice, courage, and self-control, we can improve our relationships, careers, and personal growth.

I hope this guidebook has been helpful in introducing you to Stoicism and providing practical tips for incorporating its principles into your life. Remember, the Stoic way of life is continuous practice, (so always refer back to this guidebook) not a destination, so keep striving towards your goals while living according to your values.

written by Tyronne Morrison

stoic quotes

- "We are not given a good life or a bad life. we are given life, and it's up to us to make it good or bad." - Unknown (often attributed to Confucius)

- "The greatest wealth is to live content with little." - Plato

- Difficulties strengthen the mind, as labour does the body." - Seneca

- "It is not that we have a short time to live, but that we waste a lot of it." - - Seneca

- "What upsets people is not things in themselves but their judgements about these things." - Epictetus

- "Happiness is not something ready made. It comes from your own actions." - Dalai Lama

- "Waste no more time arguing about what a good person should be. Be one." - Marcus Aurelius

- "The only way to do great work is to love what you do." - Steve Jobs

- "Wealth consists not in having great possessions, but in having few wants." - Epictetus

- "If you want to improve, be content to be thought foolish and stupid." - Epictetus

- "The happiness of your life depends upon the quality of your thoughts." - Marcus Aurelius

- "We cannot change the cards we are dealt, just how we play the hand." - Randy Pausch

- "It's not what happens to you, but how you react to it that matters." - Epictetus

- "All we have is now." - Marcus Aurelius

- "First say to yourself what you would be; and then do what you have to do." - Epictetus

- "It is in your power to withdraw yourself whenever you desire. Perfect tranquillity within consists in the good ordering of the mind, the realm of your own." - Marcus Aurelius

- "Whenever you are about to find fault with someone, ask yourself the following question: What fault of mine most nearly resembles the one I am about to criticise?" - Marcus Aurelius

- "If a man knows not what harbour he seeks, any wind is the right wind." - Seneca

- "What is not brought to consciousness, comes to us as fate." - Carl Jung

"The key is to keep company only with people who uplift you, whose presence calls forth your

Tyronne O.P Morrison

Printed in Great Britain
by Amazon

21961812R00021